AI in Medicine

Personalized Care and Optimal Outcomes

Table of Contents

1. Introduction 1

2. Understanding AI and Its Role in Modern Medicine 2

    2.1. AI: An Overview 2

    2.2. AI and Medicine: A Symbiotic Relationship 2

    2.3. Medical Diagnostics and AI 3

    2.4. AI and Patient Care 3

    2.5. AI in Surgical Procedures 4

    2.6. The Ethics of AI in Medicine 4

    2.7. Conclusion 4

3. The Science of Personalization: How AI Makes Precision
Medicine Possible 6

    3.1. The Foundations: Understanding AI and Personalized
Medicine 6

    3.2. The Process: How AI Enhances Personalized Medicine 7

    3.3. Challenges and Ethical Considerations 8

    3.4. Conclusion: AI and the Future of Personalized Medicine 9

4. Benchmarking Artificial Intelligence: Assessing its Medical
Accuracy 10

    4.1. Quantifying AI's Role in Diagnostics 10

    4.2. Clinical Decision Support Systems 11

    4.3. Prognostics and AI 11

    4.4. Precision Medicine 11

    4.5. Potential Obstacles 11

    4.6. The Way Forward 12

5. Delving into Diagnostics: AI-Enabled Medical Imaging and
Pathology 13

    5.1. The Dawn of a New Era: AI in Medical Imaging 13

    5.2. AI-Powered Radiology: Enhancing Precision Medicine 14

5.3. Machine Learning in Pathology: Increasing Diagnostic Efficiency ... 14

5.4. AI in Genomic Pathology: Towards Precision Medicine ... 15

5.5. AI-Driven Imaging Biomarkers: Predicting Patient Outcomes ... 15

6. AI in Treatment Planning: Optimizing Patient-specific Care ... 17

6.1. Role of AI in Treatment Planning ... 17

6.2. AI and Personalized Medicine ... 18

6.3. AI in Medical Imaging and Radiation Therapy ... 18

6.4. Challenges and Limitives of AI ... 19

6.5. The Future of AI in Healthcare ... 19

7. The Power of Predictive Analytics in Healthcare ... 21

7.1. Unleashing the Power of Data ... 21

7.2. Transforming Preventive Care ... 22

7.3. Enhancing Patient Outcomes ... 22

7.4. Streamlining Operations ... 22

7.5. Ensuring Cost-effectiveness ... 23

8. AI and Genomics: Pioneering Personalized Therapies ... 24

8.1. Unleashing the Power of AI in Genomics ... 24

8.2. AI-Driven Genomic Interpretation Tools ... 25

8.3. Predictive Genomics for Disease Risks ... 25

8.4. Precision Medicine and AI-Driven Genomic Analysis ... 26

8.5. Ethical and Legal Considerations ... 26

9. Artificial Intelligence in Surgical Automation ... 28

9.1. The Dawn of Surgical Automation ... 28

9.2. The Role of AI in Surgical Automation ... 28

9.3. Advancements in AI Technologies ... 29

9.4. The Integrated Digital Surgical Suite ... 29

9.5. Opportunities and Challenges ... 30

9.6. The Future of AI in Surgical Automation ... 30

10. Dealing with Data: Privacy, Security, and Ethical Concerns in AI Medicines 32

    10.1. AI, Data, and Personal Identification 32

    10.2. Patient Consent in AI Medicine 33

    10.3. Trust, Transparency, and the "Black Box" Paradox 33

    10.4. Balancing Data Access and Privacy 34

    10.5. Ethical Implications of AI Decision-Making 34

11. Future Outlook: AI's Potential to Further Revolutionize Healthcare 36

    11.1. Shaping the Future: Personalized Care 36

    11.2. Enhancing Predictive Analytics for Optimal Outcomes 37

    11.3. Rethinking Medical Imaging and Diagnosis 37

    11.4. Revolutionizing Drug Discovery and Development 38

    11.5. The Role of AI in Public Health 39

Chapter 1. Introduction

In this thought-provoking Special Report, we delve into a transformative field that is rapidly reshaping the medical landscape as we know it - Artificial Intelligence in Medicine. However, far from being an inaccessible or cumbersome read, we break the complex topic down into an engaging and intelligible narrative. With a particular focus on Personalized Care and Optimal Outcomes, we invite you to join us in exploring how AI technology is not only revolutionizing medical diagnostics and procedures, but also tailoring them to individual patient needs with unprecedented precision. Witness firsthand how these developments could enhance the efficacy of healthcare, lead to better patient outcomes, and potentially save millions of lives. Get inspired, enlightened, and make a wise decision to invest in this Special Report that is an essential read for anyone interested in the future of healthcare.

Chapter 2. Understanding AI and Its Role in Modern Medicine

Artificial intelligence (AI) has transcended its sci-fi reputation to emerge as a crucial tool for modern medicine. Defined by its ability to learn from and interpret highly complex datasets autonomously, AI is emerging as an efficient and reliable partner in various medical processes, including diagnostics, treatment planning, and patient monitoring.

2.1. AI: An Overview

AI refers to the capability of a computer system to mimic or recreate human intelligence. It is founded on algorithms that attempt to mimic the human brain's neural pathways through a framework known as neural networks. AI algorithms span different categories including machine learning (ML), deep learning, natural language processing (NLP), and more, fueling various facets within modern medicine.

AI algorithms can process vast amounts of data within moments, recognising patterns that may be invisible to the naked eye or missed in manual analysis. This makes the technology an imperative part of modern medical research and practice.

2.2. AI and Medicine: A Symbiotic Relationship

Healthcare generates an exponential amount of data on a daily basis, which necessitates an efficient method for processing and interpreting this wealth of information. From patient medical history to the latest medical research and service delivery data, there is a broad spectrum of information to be processed. AI plays a pivotal role here, dissecting this vast array of data to identify patterns, trends, and insights, transforming the future of diagnostics and treatment delivery in healthcare.

2.3. Medical Diagnostics and AI

AI algorithms are perfectly suited to detect patterns and variations in vast datasets. Many tech companies and healthcare establishments have begun to implement AI and ML models to assist medical imaging diagnosis, pathology, and genomics research. In medical imaging, AI algorithms identify and highlight abnormalities such as cancers or brain lesions which can assist doctors with diagnosis. Similarly, AI is revolutionizing pathology by interpreting images of cellular structures to identify irregularities, helping in the diagnosis and treatment planning of diseases such as cancer.

2.4. AI and Patient Care

AI's reach goes beyond diagnostics into the realm of patient care. Assisted with AI, administrative tasks are completed quickly, efficiently, and with fewer errors. Moreover, AI can predict the necessity of medical interventions, suggest personalized treatment plans, and even identify individuals who are at higher risk for certain diseases.

AI-powered chatbots are increasingly being deployed for patient monitoring and follow-up care. They can check-in with the patient, monitor their symptoms, answer basic health queries, and alert a human healthcare professional if necessary.

2.5. AI in Surgical Procedures

AI's utility extends to surgical procedures via robotic surgeries. Surgical robots can perform complex procedures with a higher level of precision than humans. They not only help to reduce human errors but also enable minimally invasive surgery and faster healing times.

While the robots are often controlled by human surgeons, Machine Learning algorithms play a pivotal role in assisting, learning from each procedure, and improving over time.

2.6. The Ethics of AI in Medicine

While AI offers great potential in reshaping healthcare, ethical guidelines need to be established for its use. Issues such as patient consent, data privacy, and algorithmic bias need to be addressed. There have been cases where AI systems incorporated biases present in their training data, leading to disparate healthcare outcomes for different demographic groups.

Additionally, AI's reliance on data poses a challenge to patient privacy. As AI requires vast quantities of medical data to function effectively, it's crucial to strike a balance between leveraging data and protecting patient privacy.

2.7. Conclusion

No technological development is without its challenges, and AI is no exception. Its potential to revolutionize medicine is exceptional, but care must be taken to mitigate its associated risks. Yet, given the rapid advancements in this sector, the promise for a healthier, more efficient future in healthcare imbued with AI seems not a matter of 'if' but 'when'.

Overall, AI's application in modern medicine is testament to human ingenuity, our commitment to improve lives and optimize healthcare outcomes. As we continue to develop and fine-tune these models, it's anticipated that AI will become even more entrenched in medical diagnostics and patient care strategies, promising an exciting future for health service delivery. In the coming era of medicine, embracing AI may indeed become a non-negotiable for providing optimal care.

Chapter 3. The Science of Personalization: How AI Makes Precision Medicine Possible

AI in medicine has opened up new realms of possibilities that vary remarkably in terms of precision and efficacy. The amalgamation of data-driven practices with cutting-edge technology can redefine several paradigms of the healthcare sector, particularly in the aspect of personalized medicine, where treatments are adapted to each patient's specific needs and attributes.

3.1. The Foundations: Understanding AI and Personalized Medicine

The term "Artificial Intelligence" encompasses a cluster of technologies, including machine learning (ML), natural language processing (NLP), speech recognition, and computer vision. These technologies, founded on the principle that systems can perform tasks without being explicitly programmed to do so, are geared to mimic human intelligence.

On the other hand, personalized medicine refers to tailoring medical treatment to the individual characteristics, needs, and preferences of each patient. Personalized medicine, backed by genomics and proteomics, allows for therapies to be custom-made for each patient's unique genetic, biochemical, and physiological makeup.

Combining these two potent forces - AI and personalization -

introduces an era of precision medicine that promises nothing short of a paradigm shift in healthcare. AI's ability to process and interpret vast and diverse datasets, including electronic health records, genomic data, and even medical literature, gives it the necessary tools to deliver personalized medicine in a manner that was unimaginable until recently.

3.2. The Process: How AI Enhances Personalized Medicine

AI technology facilitates the delivery of personalized medicine by leveraging large and varied data sources, generating insights that could lead to more accurate diagnoses and ultimately better health outcomes for patients.

To begin with, AI technology can help in disease identification and analysis. Using a variety of data, from medical history to genetic markers, AI systems can predict disease risk more accurately than traditional methods. This enhanced ability to predict health outcomes aids in better tailoring treatments to individual patients.

Moreover, AI can aid in data analysis and treatment plans. It can consider an enormous range of factors that may impact a patient's health status, including their genetic predispositions, medical history, lifestyle, and demographics. Combining these factors, AI algorithms can provide highly personalized and efficient treatment plans.

Lastly, AI can enable personalized drug delivery systems. AI-driven systems have the potential to design customized drugs based on a patient's unique medical profile. As a result, these personalized drugs provide better treatment outcomes, reduce the risk of adverse drug reactions, and ensure optimal drug efficacy, posing great potential for patient wellbeing and cost savings.

3.3. Challenges and Ethical Considerations

While there's undoubtedly extraordinary potential in applying AI to personalized medicine, there are serious challenges and ethical considerations surrounding its deployment. These revolve around data privacy, the transparency of AI models, the reliability of AI-driven diagnosis, biased algorithms, and the risk of misuse.

Data privacy is a significant concern, given the extremely sensitive nature of the data involved in personalized medicine. There needs to be robust infrastructure and stringent regulations to protect this data.

The "black box" phenomenon in AI, where the workings of an AI model are not transparent or understandable to humans, may also pose substantial problems. In a medical context, these opaque systems can lead to mistrust and skepticism among patients and healthcare providers alike.

Further, while AI has made significant strides in diagnosing diseases, the technology is not yet foolproof. Misdiagnostic issues could lead to incorrect treatments, causing harm to patients.

In terms of biased algorithms, AI models trained on non-representative data can produce biased outputs. This can lead to health disparities and inequality.

Lastly, the malicious use of AI and personalized medicine information raises significant ethical concerns. The potential for misuse of this information for nefarious purposes is a significant threat that must be guarded against.

3.4. Conclusion: AI and the Future of Personalized Medicine

Artificial Intelligence is transforming the way we approach medicine and healthcare. While it is not without its difficulties, the potential of AI to improve and personalize patient care is overwhelmingly positive.

The opportunity to marshal this technology to predict disease risk better, enhance treatment plans, and implement personalized drug delivery systems can revolutionize the landscape of healthcare. With careful oversight and stringent ethical frameworks in place, AI-powered personalized medicine has the ability to redefine the contours of medical practice to the benefit of us all.

This journey is just beginning. Like the human genome project, which exponentially accelerated the rate of genetic discoveries, AI has the potential to drive personalized medicine into a new era of discovery, development, and delivery. As we pour more knowledge into this burgeoning field, we are likely to see more complex and incredible intersections of AI and personalized medicine in the future. It's an exciting time for medicine and healthcare, and we are privileged to be part of this journey.

Chapter 4. Benchmarking Artificial Intelligence: Assessing its Medical Accuracy

The global approach to patient diagnostics, prognostics, and therapeutics has been greatly influenced by the advent of artificial intelligence (AI), underpinned by machine learning. The relentless surge of algorithm use in medical accuracy is a direct testimony to its transformative strength.

4.1. Quantifying AI's Role in Diagnostics

The realm of diagnostics, traditionally reliant on the subjective scrutiny of medical imaging by radiologists, is being revolutionized by the advent of AI. Machine learning utilizes algorithms that learn from existing high-volume medical imaging data and make precise predictions. This eliminates human error and accelerates the diagnostic process significantly. A recent study demonstrated AI's advantage over human analysis in detecting breast cancer in mammography with a reduced rate of false negatives by 9.4% and false positives by 5.7%.

AI diagnostics is not limited to radiology. Pathologists are leveraging machine learning in detecting abnormalities in biopsy samples, while cardiologists use it to identify congenital heart defects. McKinsey estimates that AI could help diagnose up to 50% diseases that are currently un-diagnosed, fundamentally transforming the diagnostic landscape.

4.2. Clinical Decision Support Systems

These systems offer healthcare providers recommendations based on patient-specific information. They use sophisticated algorithms integrating all available data, including patient history, lifestyle, genetic factors, and population health data. A study comparing the performance of AI clinical decision support system with expert-level physicians found that the system made accurate diagnoses in 87% of cases, while human practitioners reached correct conclusions in 86% of cases.

4.3. Prognostics and AI

AI is also providing groundbreaking insights in predicting disease progression, telegraphing individual patients' future health risks. Its effectiveness in data analysis heralds a new era of personalized forecast reports correlating lifestyle, genetic predispositions, and environmental factors to predict disease trajectories.

4.4. Precision Medicine

Aimed at tailoring treatment to individual genetic profiles, precision medicine exploits AI in identifying patterns and correlations in complex genomic data. Aided by machine learning, researchers are unraveling how genetic variations contribute to individual responses to different treatments. This is being used to guide pharmaceutical development, create personalized therapies, and improve drug delivery methods.

4.5. Potential Obstacles

Not without challenges, the incorporation of AI in medicine brings ethical, legal, and data integrity issues. Concerns stem from issues of accountability when AI-related medical errors occur, patient privacy in data handling, and the lack of knowledge about how AI reaches its conclusions. The question of regulating AI technologies also remains contentious.

4.6. The Way Forward

Despite hurdles, there's a global consensus on the transformative potential of AI in healthcare. Encouragingly, healthcare systems are acclimating to this change through strategic investment and agnostic regulations. Governing bodies and stakeholders are discussing ethical standards, deliberating legislation regarding AI implementation, and reassessing educational curricula to include the interdisciplinary study of applied AI.

AI is indisputably creating seismic shifts in healthcare, altering both patient care dynamics and clinical workflow. It harbors promise for optimal outcomes with personalized care plans, early diagnosis, accurate prognosis, and tailored therapies. Human and algorithmic intelligence are not competing in this setting; instead, they are synergistically collaborating to redefine the way we view and administer healthcare.

In conclusion, the accuracy and efficiency brought by AI in medicine, though benchmarked against traditional measures, are ushering in a new era of superlative healthcare standards. Continued investment in AI technologies, collaborative learning, and robust regulatory norms could elevate this revolution, transforming it into a healthcare mainstay, and possibly a conduit to the elusive panacea of all times.

Chapter 5. Delving into Diagnostics: AI-Enabled Medical Imaging and Pathology

Artificial Intelligence is forging ahead at a blistering pace, moulding the medical diagnostics landscape by intertwining data and technology to deliver more accurate, faster results than ever before. As we tread further into this paradigm-shifting revolution, our aim is to enlighten you about how AI-powered tools are redefining medical imaging and pathology.

5.1. The Dawn of a New Era: AI in Medical Imaging

Medical imaging, an indispensible aspect of modern healthcare, is undergoing a seismic evolution with AI at its helm. Today, we are witnessing the integration of AI techniques like machine learning and deep learning in advanced imaging modalities like MRI, CT, Ultrasound and X-rays. The goal - to augment speed, accuracy, and precision in diagnosis.

Machine learning algorithms are trained to recognize patterns in imaging data, significantly reducing the time taken to report findings. For instance, AI radiology tools can locate a fracture or detect a pulmonary nodule significantly faster than traditional methods. The power of AI lies not just in acceleration, but in its potential to combat the problem of shortage of trained technicians and radiologists. With AI moderating routine screening, resources can be focused more productively, increasing efficiency of healthcare delivery.

5.2. AI-Powered Radiology: Enhancing Precision Medicine

Let's delve into this chapter's first instance of how AI can personalize and optimize care - radiology. The role of AI in medical imaging immensely contributes to the advancement of Precision Medicine, a medical model promoting prevention and treatment strategies custom-made for individual patients.

Modern AI-powered radiology techniques are designed to aid radiologists in accurately diagnosing conditions such as lung, brain, and breast cancer. Variances between different scans, which could be missed by the human eye, can be effectively identified by AI algorithms. Accordingly, AI's ability to recognize patterns in imaging data is also being leveraged for predicting treatment response and clinical outcomes, thereby guiding personalized therapy plans. This approach forms the crux of Precision Medicine, and AI is poised to be its major contributor.

5.3. Machine Learning in Pathology: Increasing Diagnostic Efficiency

Now, it's time to shift our focus from medical imaging to another significant aspect of diagnostics - pathology. Pathology, often described as the cornerstone of most diagnostics, has also been positively disrupted by AI.

Machine learning tools are being used to scan many histopathological slides at once, reducing time and improving accuracy in diagnosis. Rather than replacing pathologists, AI supports them by helping identify critical morphological features easily missed by the human eye.

5.4. AI in Genomic Pathology: Towards Precision Medicine

Genomic pathology, the study of disease from a genetic standpoint, is a burgeoning field positioned at the nexus of pathology and genomics. With the inclusion of AI, we are seeing transformative breakthroughs in this domain.

AI can effectively analyze genetic patterns, contributing significantly to the concept of Personalized Medicine. Machine learning algorithms can detect gene mutations associated with certain diseases and help predict disease susceptibility in individuals, thereby helping clinicians to design patient-specific preventative interventions. Furthermore, AI holds immense potential in therapeutic guidance for patients, especially in the arena of cancer treatment where individual genetic makeup can determine the suitable course of action.

5.5. AI-Driven Imaging Biomarkers: Predicting Patient Outcomes

A key role that AI plays in diagnostic imaging is discovery and evaluation of imaging biomarkers. These biomarkers provide valuable information about disease characteristics and prognosis, guiding the preferred course of treatment.

AI algorithms can analyze numerous imaging characteristics and their combinations in a fraction of time as compared to manual inspection, identifying potential imaging biomarkers that help predict patient outcomes. Using these biomarkers, clinicians can tailor treatments, monitoring response and adjusting strategies as needed, to ensure optimal patient outcomes - a perfect example of Personalized Care.

To sum it up, the integration of AI in diagnostics is a promising development that is poised to radically transform the healthcare landscape. It incentivizes personalized care, improves the efficiency and accuracy of diagnoses, and ultimately, enhances patient outcomes. Investing in the advancement and application of AI in diagnostics is not just an investment in technology; it's an investment in the future of healthcare and in human lives. This detailed exposition is merely a sneak peak into this transformative field; the extensive potential that lies ahead is boundless, unlocked by expanding our knowledge and embracing the power of AI.

Chapter 6. AI in Treatment Planning: Optimizing Patient-specific Care

Artificial intelligence (AI) plays a pivotal role in transforming how medical treatment planning is undertaken, enabling a personalization of care that optimizes patient-specific outcomes. Like an experienced medical practitioner, AI can sift through voluminous data, discern patterns, and make predictions. However, it performs these tasks at an unmatched speed and scale, opening doors to new possibilities in patient care.

6.1. Role of AI in Treatment Planning

AI's most prominent role in treatment planning revolves around its ability to interpret and draw valuable conclusions from vast, complex data sets. For patients, this means a highly personalized diagnosis and treatment, rooted in a comprehensive understanding of their unique genetic makeup and lifestyle factors.

Predictive analytics, a branch of AI, uses machine learning algorithms to forecast future events based on historical data. In the realm of medicine, this capability is invaluable. Predictive analytics can estimate the likelihood of disease recurrence, enabling practitioners to adjust treatment plans proactively and potentially prevent adverse events. This proactive approach provides an immense value in diseases like cancer, where early detection and prevention contribute significantly to the patient's survival and quality of life.

6.2. AI and Personalized Medicine

Personalized medicine is the customization of healthcare - medical decisions, practices, and treatments are tailored to individual patients. Central to this concept is pharmacogenomics- the study of how genes affect a person's response to drugs. AI greatly aids in applying pharmacogenomics to inform patient-specific treatment plans.

Pharmacogenomic data are complex, comprising information from myriad genes and their numerous mutations. Interpreting this data with traditional methods is slow, labor-intensive, and often yields incomplete results. Conversely, AI-powered systems can quickly analyze this data, identifying gene-drug interactions that may impact a patient's response to treatment. This capability allows healthcare providers to select medications and dosages best suited to an individual's genetic profile, increasing the effectiveness of treatment and minimizing adverse drug reactions.

Additionally, AI's ability to analyze vast databases of clinical trial data allows it to match patients with ongoing clinical trials that could potentially benefit their treatment. Targeted therapies, gene therapies, or yet unapproved treatment options could all offer avenues for improved outcomes. Thus, AI not only personalizes care but gives patients access to the latest innovations.

6.3. AI in Medical Imaging and Radiation Therapy

AI's role in medical imaging and radiation therapy is two-fold. On the one hand, it optimizes diagnosis through improved image analysis. On the other, it refines radiation treatment plans by identifying the most effective delivery route.

AI can detect minute differences in medical scans that might be overlooked by the human eye, making it indispensable in early disease detection. In radiation therapy, AI algorithms can analyze a patient's scans to determine the optimal radiation dose, angles, and delivery routes, reducing the impact on healthy surrounding tissue while ensuring maximal damage to cancer cells.

6.4. Challenges and Limitives of AI

Despite its potential, AI's integration into medical treatment planning faces many challenges. There are concerns about data privacy, as AI algorithms require vast quantities of patient health data. Health professionals must assiduously protect this data, a task made more difficult by complex healthcare systems, and data sharing mechanisms.

Another challenge is the risk of algorithmic bias influencing decision-making. AI algorithms learn from the data they're given, and if that data is biased, it may produce biased results, leading to inequality in healthcare delivery.

Artificial intelligence, while extraordinarily powerful, lacks the human touch. It can analyze data and make predictions, but it cannot understand the emotional and psychosocial aspects of a patient's condition. Such understanding is vital to medical decision-making and must come from a health professional's human empathy.

Despite these challenges, AI's role in optimizing patient-specific care remains promising. It is a powerful tool that, utilized conscientiously, can result in enhanced patient care and improved health outcomes. It is anticipated that as AI evolves and data privacy measures become more robust, many of these pressing concerns will be mitigated.

6.5. The Future of AI in Healthcare

The future of AI in the healthcare sector is ripe with opportunities.

Machine learning algorithms will become even more precise and powerful, bolstering their predictive and prescriptive capabilities. As AI technologies continue to evolve, it is anticipated that clinicians worldwide will adopt AI tools for diagnosis, treatment planning, risk prediction, patient monitoring, and more.

In the future, AI has the potential to become a standard tool in the arsenal of healthcare professionals. Like every innovative form of technology, it requires continuous research and cautious application. It may not be a panacea for all healthcare issues, but AI will doubtlessly play a significant role in advancing patient-specific care, ultimately bettering the health and lives of patients everywhere.

As AI continues to evolve and reshape the medical landscape, so too should our approach to integrating this technology into our healthcare systems. Only then can we maximize the potential benefits and use AI to truly meet individual patient needs, promoting optimal health outcomes for all.

Chapter 7. The Power of Predictive Analytics in Healthcare

Predictive analytics, at its core, is the use of data, statistical algorithms, and machine learning techniques to identify the likelihood of future outcomes based on historical data. In the realm of healthcare, it extends its applications to forecast outbreaks of epidemics, avoid preventable diseases, reduce costs of treatment, predict inpatient admission rates and improve the quality of life.

7.1. Unleashing the Power of Data

Healthcare institutions generate massive amounts of data daily, including patient records, medical images, lab results and genomics data. This data, if accurately analyzed and interpreted, can offer actionable insights to healthcare professionals. Predictive analytics uses this data to recognize patterns and make predictions about future healthcare outcomes. The artificial intelligence (AI) algorithms can be trained on millions of data points to recognize patterns and make predictions about the future events which a human would miss.

AI-enabled predictive analysis allows for a more proactive approach to healthcare. Providers can now predict with a high degree of accuracy the likelihood of certain diseases developing or progressing. This is monumental in reducing healthcare costs by allowing for early interventions and efficient resource management. It opens the door for personalized care since the diagnosis and treatment methodologies can be tailored to suit each patient's unique genetic make-up and lifestyle.

7.2. Transforming Preventive Care

Preventive care is one of the most effective ways to reduce the burden of chronic diseases. Predictive analytics aids in the identification of high-risk patient groups who are likely to benefit from preventive measures. Health systems and insurers can use predictive analytics to target these populations with relevant preventive screenings and treatments.

Moreover, data related to social determinants of health, such as living conditions and socioeconomic status, can be coupled with traditional health data to generate comprehensive risk profiles. This facilitates early interventions, reducing the necessity for expensive treatments and hospitalizations and improving overall population health.

7.3. Enhancing Patient Outcomes

Predictive analytics helps to understand the risks associated with different treatments, paving the way for patient-centric care. For example, in cancer care, data-driven predictions can help doctors choose the most effective treatment plan and minimize the harmful side effects.

Moreover, predictive analytics can assist in better management of chronic illnesses such as diabetes or heart disease. By utilizing patient data like blood glucose levels, genetic information, and lifestyle habits, predictive models can set off alarms when there's a heightened risk of a potentially harmful event such as a heart attack allowing for early and proactive care.

7.4. Streamlining Operations

Healthcare providers can utilize predictive analytics to optimize operational efficiency in terms of staffing, bed management and equipment utilization. It can be used to predict patient admission rates, length of hospital stays and discharge dates, enabling resource allocation to be planned in advance, reducing costs and ensuring a more streamlined experience for patients.

Furthermore, during situations such as the recent COVID-19 pandemic, predictive analytics has played a crucial role in managing resources. It has provided valuable insights into shock trends, the need for hospital beds, ventilators, and PPE - thus enabling better crisis management.

7.5. Ensuring Cost-effectiveness

The rise of value-based care models has underlined the need for cost-effectiveness in healthcare. Predictive analytics plays a key role in eliminating unnecessary expenses. It assists in identifying redundant tests, reducing hospital readmissions, and facilitating precision medicine that can help avoid costly trial-and-error treatment approaches.

In conclusion, the power of predictive analytics in healthcare is immense. It enables healthcare providers to deliver efficient, personalized, and cost-effective care. It allows for better disease prevention, management and treatment strategies that can advance people's health and longevity. While concerns about data privacy and integration are genuine, with strategic planning, robust data governance policies, and continuous technological advancements, predictive analytics promises to be a game-changing force in healthcare.

Chapter 8. AI and Genomics: Pioneering Personalized Therapies

Artificial Intelligence (AI) and Genomics have emerged at the forefront of personalized therapies, unlocking a new horizon in medical science. Merging the unparalleled strength of AI with the wealth of insights present in the genomic data holds the promise to bring about a revolution in personalized care and optimize treatment outcomes.

8.1. Unleashing the Power of AI in Genomics

Sophisticated machine learning algorithms today offer remarkable capabilities in examining and interpreting the vast ocean of genomic data. Powered by artificial intelligence, these algorithms can identify patterns and correlations in genomic sequences which otherwise would be a daunting task for clinicians.

Genomic sequencing generates a torrent of data which can be challenging to handle and interpret. Traditional methods that involve manual intervention can lead to potential human error and are time-consuming. However, with the advent of AI, researchers can easily navigate through billions of DNA sequences and unravel hidden genetic anomalies with unparalleled speed and accuracy.

The "genome-wide association studies" (GWAS) provide a prime example of how AI can enhance genomics. These studies involve scanning markers across complete sets of DNA, or genomes, of many individuals to find genetic variations associated with a particular disease. AI can analyze these large volumes of genomic data, expediting the discovery of genetic syndromes and mutations associated with disease onset and progression. This has tremendous implications for early disease detection and the provision of personalized treatments.

8.2. AI-Driven Genomic Interpretation Tools

Several innovative tools have surfaced in recent years, using AI and machine learning to analyze and interpret genomic data for personalized therapies. These tools offer capabilities such as predicting gene regulation, identifying disease-causing mutations, and suggesting potential therapeutic interventions.

DeepVariant, developed by Google, is one such tool that employs deep learning to make more accurate predictions about genetic variants. It has shown remarkable performance in interpreting genetic mutations that might contribute to disease conditions.

Another application is Fabric Genomics's AI platform, capable of rapidly interpreting genomic data and applying it to patient care. It uses AI to analyze whole genome sequencing data and identify variants associated with genetic diseases, helping clinicians provide the most effective, personalized treatments.

8.3. Predictive Genomics for Disease Risks

One of the most significant advances brought by AI in Genomics is its role in predicting disease risks. By examining DNA sequences, AI models can identify genetic markers associated with various diseases, such as cancer, cardiovascular disorders, and neurological conditions, among others.

AI can predict an individual's lifetime risk of developing a specific condition by considering multiple genetic factors in tandem with environmental and lifestyle factors. For example, using machine learning algorithms, Polly, an AI developed by Insitro, examines genomic datasets to assess disease risk, enabling preventative interventions and early treatments.

8.4. Precision Medicine and AI-Driven Genomic Analysis

The synergy of AI with Genomics paves the path towards precision medicine - a novel healthcare approach where medical decisions, treatments, and preventive strategies are tailored to the individual patient's genetic profile.

The precision oncology platform developed by Tempus, for instance, uses AI to analyze molecular and clinical data and design personalized treatment plans for cancer patients. It identifies therapeutic options targeting the molecular alterations in each patient's tumor, potentially improving treatment efficacy and patient outcome.

8.5. Ethical and Legal Considerations

As we push the boundaries of AI and Genomics, it becomes crucial to consider ethical and legal implications. Issues surrounding genetic data privacy, informed consent for genetic testing, and equitable access to personalized therapies take center stage.

Responsible use of AI in Genomics requires ethical practices and robust legal protections while ensuring accessibility and broad benefit. Genetic data privacy must be robustly protected, and consent procedures for genetic testing should be clear and comprehensive.

In conclusion, the blend of AI and Genomics carries immense potential to transform personalized therapies. It holds a promising future in healthcare, promising more precise diagnoses, improved treatment planning, and a move towards more anticipatory and preventive healthcare. However, to unlock its full potential, more research, concerted effort in integrating AI into genomics practice, and thoughtful ethical considerations are required.

Chapter 9. Artificial Intelligence in Surgical Automation

The transformative advent of Artificial Intelligence (AI) is progressively permeating every sub-sector of healthcare, with one of the most profound implications being seen in the field of surgical automation.

9.1. The Dawn of Surgical Automation

The landscape of surgery has witnessed massive strides over the past few decades, and recent innovations have been primarily driven by robotics and AI. Surgical robots are no longer novelties but have become an integral part of operating rooms worldwide. Typical robotic surgical systems contain three key parts: a console where the surgeon sits and controls the robot, a patient-side cart where the robot interacts with the patient, and a high-definition 3D vision system. However, AI takes this a step further, opening the door for fully autonomous surgical robots capable of functioning with minimal human intervention.

9.2. The Role of AI in Surgical Automation

The integration of AI in surgical robotics aims to improve surgical outcomes significantly, by providing unparalleled precision and consistency, minimizing human error, reducing fatigue, and increasing the surgeon's ability to perform complex procedures. Through sophisticated algorithms and machine learning, these systems can harness their extensive database of past surgeries to inform real-time decision-making, thereby adapting the surgical technique not just to the presenting condition but also to the patient's unique anatomy.

9.3. Advancements in AI Technologies

Deep learning, one of the core methodologies of AI, has shown particular promise within this sphere. By utilizing layered artificial neural networks, these systems can learn from a vast collection of annotated surgical videos, teaching themselves to recognize specific anatomical structures, surgical tools, and interpret different surgical gestures. Furthermore, AI systems can predict potential complications based on the real-time analysis of patient vitals, such as heart rate, blood pressure, and oxygen consumption, allowing the surgical team to adapt their strategy accordingly.

Another notable development is Reinforcement Learning (RL). In RL, an agent learns to perform tasks by interacting with an environment, improving by maximizing certain aspects of a reward signal. Robot-assisted surgeries often involve a large number of complex, yet well-defined actions which makes RL a perfect match for this application.

9.4. The Integrated Digital Surgical Suite

In fully embracing this AI-driven future, the concept of the 'Integrated Digital Surgical Suite' has been developed. This suite encompasses a wide range of features including pre-operative imaging studies, an intra-operative surgical guidance system, and post-operative monitoring technologies. Here, patient data and imaging studies are continuously assessed and synchronized with the surgical robot's movements in real-time. By integrating and streamlining data processing, errors can be caught before they occur, surgical plans can be adjusted dynamically, and patients can be accurately monitored post-operatively, reducing the risk of complications.

9.5. Opportunities and Challenges

There are also several challenges in shifting towards AI-powered surgical automation. The biggest hurdles are related to the transparency of AI decisions, possible machine malfunction, and the legal and ethical considerations in the event of complications or surgery-related injuries. Questions about the responsibility in case of AI-driven surgical malpractice are yet to be adequately addressed.

Despite these challenges, the potential benefits of AI in surgical automation are too significant to be ignored. Unprecedented accuracy, superior patient outcomes and efficiencies in healthcare processes represent a compelling case for the integration of AI in surgical environments.

9.6. The Future of AI in Surgical Automation

Looking forward, the horizon of surgical automation glimmers with promise as AI continues to evolve. With the foundations now established, the advent of intelligent automation suggests that robots may soon not only assist surgeons but also perform tasks independently. As technological advancements continue to push the boundaries of AI, and as these systems learn, adapt, and improve, the realm of possibilities in surgical automation continues to expand. The future of AI-assisted surgery is not just promising; it's beginning to take shape.

AI in surgical automation is undoubtedly revolutionizing healthcare, and this evolution has only just begun. We stand on the precipice of a new era in medicine, one where AI doesn't replace human doctors but works alongside them, augmenting their capabilities, minimizing errors, and ensuring optimal patient outcomes. It's an exciting time, and the prospects are limitless. As we continue this exploration, it becomes increasingly clear that to invest in AI is to invest in the future of healthcare itself.

Chapter 10. Dealing with Data: Privacy, Security, and Ethical Concerns in AI Medicines

The rapid proliferation of AI in medicine is undeniably transforming the landscape of healthcare, enabling enhanced diagnostics, personalized treatment, and improved outcomes. However, with this promise comes a multitude of privacy, data security, and ethical challenges. This detailed exploration of the subject matter underlines the essential steps to overcoming these concerns while realizing the enormous potential of this burgeoning field.

10.1. AI, Data, and Personal Identification

At the heart of medical AI is data, with countless records of diagnoses, medical images, patient demographics, and even genetic information being utilized to feed and train AI systems. Each of these data points potentially carries the risk of personal identification. In accordance with data protection legislation, healthcare providers must ensure that data is processed and stored in ways that prevent identification of individuals.

Pseudonymization, a method that replaces identifying fields within a data record with artificial identifiers (or pseudonyms), has been implemented by many institutions. While this allows essential information to be retained for analysis, even this comes with its own potential pitfalls. Highly sophisticated AI systems may still be able to reconstruct identities by cross-referencing multiple information sources, inferring connections, and teasing out revealing patterns.

Solutions for such issues are being researched, such as advanced data anonymization techniques. Some are looking to homomorphic encryption, a form of cryptography that enables computation on ciphertexts, generating encrypted results which, when decrypted, match the result of operations performed on the plaintext. This means, AI could work on anonymized data without ever needing to access private information.

10.2. Patient Consent in AI Medicine

Consent becomes a more complex issue with AI in medicine. Whereas traditionally, healthcare professionals informed patients about their specific treatments, with AI systems, an entirely new level of transparency is required.

Ideally, the patient should understand how AI is used to assist in their treatment and what type of data it employs. Would patients need to consent every time their data is used to train, test, or run an AI model? Or is an initial general consent sufficient? Furthermore, since AI models continually learn and adapt, how often should consent be renewed?

Here, the formation of practical consent models and ethically robust policy frameworks is key. The ongoing dialogues should seek to strike a balance, weighing the benefits of AI with the need to respect patient autonomy.

10.3. Trust, Transparency, and the "Black Box" Paradox

The "black box" issue refers to the lack of transparency and understanding of how AI algorithms make decisions. This can undermine trust and ethical decision-making in healthcare settings.

Concrete steps should be adopted to make AI algorithms in medicine as transparent and explainable as possible. Strategies may involve implementing "white box" algorithms that are more understandable by design or developing ways to "interpret" black box algorithms.

Among the efforts aimed at this problem are Explainable AI (XAI) projects. These aim to create AI that can not only excel at tasks but also explain its reasoning in understandable terms to human operators.

10.4. Balancing Data Access and Privacy

To function effectively, AI in medicine requires large amounts of data. However, an enormous balancing act is needed to ensure that privacy is maintained without crippling the transformative potential of AI.

Centralized databases pose a risk of breaches, with high-value medical data a tempting target for hackers. Decentralization and cryptography can help, but they also present challenges for data access and AI training.

A possible solution being touted is federated learning, an approach where AI algorithms are sent to the location of the data, trained locally, and then the learnings (not the data) returned to the central server. This ensures the data remains in control of the original institution, hence providing an extra layer of security.

10.5. Ethical Implications of AI Decision-Making

AI, with its ability to predict diagnoses and suggest treatments, introduces an unprecedented level of decision-making capability that directly impacts patient life. Questions of accountability, bias in training data, and interpretability of decisions arise in such scenarios. Mitigating these challenges demands ensuring that every deployed AI system has been tested for fairness, understandability, robustness, and reliability.

In conclusion, while AI in medicine offers remarkable promise for improved healthcare, it is incumbent upon all stakeholders to address the challenges of data privacy, security, and ethics. A robust regulatory framework, advanced technologies, and clear ethical guidelines will all be part of the solution as we navigate this new era of medical technology. Care must also be taken to nurture trust between AI and its human users, patients, and healthcare professionals alike. Only through such prudence can AI fulfill its potential as a life-saving tool in medicine.

Chapter 11. Future Outlook: AI's Potential to Further Revolutionize Healthcare

The rollout of Artificial Intelligence in the medical field has been swift, expedited by the intricate needs of modern healthcare. As technologists and medical professionals work hand-in-hand to improve diagnostics, treatment rites, and patient outcomes, we can safely predict that AI's influence on healthcare will only deepen. This chapter contemplates the role of AI in the near and distant future of healthcare.

11.1. Shaping the Future: Personalized Care

One of the most significant advantages of AI in medicine is the potential for personalized care. AI algorithms can process vast quantities of patient data to detect underlying patterns that humans might miss. These patterns can reveal not only a more accurate diagnosis but also a prognosis tailored to the individual's lifestyle, genetic makeup, and overall health.

Current research indicates AI's immense potential in this area. Studies show AI's ability to provide personalized predictions and treatments for diseases like cancer, heart disease, and diabetes. The future may see algorithms that can combine genomic, clinical, and lifestyle data to give precise health predictions and customized treatments.

AI in personalized care could lead to a paradigm shift from generalized healthcare, centered on population-level data, to an individual-centric model. The main consequence of this shift would be a significant increase in treatment effectiveness, as treatments would be customized to the patient's genetic markers and personal health data.

11.2. Enhancing Predictive Analytics for Optimal Outcomes

The healthcare industry relies heavily on prediction, but conventional models often lack accuracy. AI's potential to enhance predictive analytics is therefore considerable. AI-powered predictive models could forecast patient deterioration, disease outbreak, readmission likelihood, and more with unprecedented accuracy.

AI predictive models are already being used in specific applications. For instance, Google's DeepMind developed an AI-based early warning system that predicts acute kidney injury 48 hours before it occurs. AI's predictive prowess will also be instrumental in managing infectious disease outbreaks, preparing healthcare systems for population-level emergencies.

Predictive analytics will become increasingly crucial as healthcare systems transition to value-based care models, where reimbursement is linked to patient outcomes. AI models will enable clinicians to accurately predict how patients will respond to treatments, leading to optimal patient outcomes.

11.3. Rethinking Medical Imaging and Diagnosis

Medical images are central to disease diagnosis. However, interpreting these images is no easy feat and has traditionally been susceptible to human error. AI algorithms have shown impressive results in improving the diagnosis from medical images.

Machine learning models have been utilized in diagnosing conditions such as lung cancer, breast cancer, and Alzheimer's disease from imaging data with potentially even greater precision than human radiologists. In the future, AI could become a staple tool in diagnostic radiology, drastically reducing diagnostic error and improving early disease detection.

AI technology can also revolutionize pathology by automating disease detection from biopsy images. PathAI, a platform for automated pathological diagnosis, has shown promise in improving diagnostic accuracy and reducing reading times.

11.4. Revolutionizing Drug Discovery and Development

Drug discovery is one of the most time-consuming and expensive processes in medicine. AI has the potential to expedite drug discovery by mapping disease pathways, predicting drug-target interactions, and optimizing drug design.

AI algorithms can scan biomedical literature to identify potential drug targets and predict how drugs interact with these targets. They can also generate drug candidates by simulating molecular properties. In the future, these capabilities could significantly reduce the time and capital needed to bring new drugs to market.

One noteworthy example is the AI system developed by Google's DeepMind called 'AlphaFold,' which can predict protein structures with remarkable accuracy. This development could revolutionize drug discovery, as understanding protein structures is critical for developing therapeutics as they are often the targets of medication.

11.5. The Role of AI in Public Health

From disease tracking to predicting and preventing outbreaks, AI has the potential to revolutionize public health. AI can synthesize diverse data sources such as clinical records, social media posts, and satellite images to generate real-time insights into public health trends.

AI algorithms are already used in outbreak tracking. One example is BlueDot, a platform that successfully predicted the global spread of the COVID-19 pandemic. The future may see more sophisticated AI systems for public health surveillance, enabling quick responses to disease outbreaks and other health emergencies.

In conclusion, the impact of AI on healthcare is only beginning to unravel. Everything from personalized care to drug discovery could be revolutionized. AI's power to process vast amounts of data could lead to healthcare that is more predictive, proactive, and personalized. This shift could improve care quality, outcome, and access, heralding a new era in healthcare. Despite the obstacles and ethical considerations involved, the benefits of such a paradigm shift far outweigh the potential downsides.